LEARN ARABIC FOR BEGINNERS

500+ Common Arabic Vocabulary
and Useful Phrases for Your Visit to Egypt

Shuk Institute

TABLE OF CONTENTS

REVIEW

Thank you for purchasing this book. If you happen to find it helpful in anyway, make sure you head over to Amazon and leave a review about your experience. We would love to hear how your communication in Arabic unfolded with this book in your hands.

ABOUT THE BOOK

This book is a quick guide that introduces the reader to the Arabic language right from its core. It covers a brief history of Arabic and takes the reader through the language from the basic syllables to more than 500 basic vocabulary and phrases, which the reader can use daily.

Reading this book will enable English speakers who are beginners to learn and speak Arabic effectively in no time.

By the end of this book, the learner will be introduced to 500+ basic vocabulary and phrases in Arabic, their English translation and transliteration using English letters and sounds to facilitate the learning process. In addition, the transliterations are written in Egyptian dialect and allows the reader to enjoy a cloudless learning experience where all sounds are evident and purely expressed.

WHO IS THIS BOOK FOR?

This book is highly recommended to any English speakers that are specifically visiting Egypt and want to learn Arabic. Since the Egyptian Arabic dialect is common and popular around the world, this book will still be useful in any Arabic speaking country. Whether you would like to learn Arabic because you find it an interesting language or like to learn Arabic for education or business-related purposes, this guide is for you!

The book offers both: theoretical and practical knowledge of the Arabic language. Therefore, it is perfect assistance for students visiting Arabic-speaking countries for education or business delegate trips. The book also caters for all age groups who wish to learn Arabic.

The book is authored from basic Arabic history to practical scenarios through basic language knowledge. Its content, therefore, helps the reader grasp the language basics and communicate through various phrases for various situations.

"To speak a language is to take on a world, a culture."

-     Frantz Fanon

INTRODUCTION

The Arabic language could be traced back to the Bantu family of African languages. It is defined as a family since all languages related to this family share some remarkable features peculiar to this family alone. In a sense, these features may or may not be found in other families, and regardless of whether these families are in the same geographical scope or not.

In a sense, the most striking feature of the Bantu family is that every word referring to any concept in the known universe is divided into classes, which includes but is not limited to having the same source of the word to form the remaining word classes. For example, in English, when discussing food and beverages, the word eat – by the simplest definition of word as a set of letters – has nothing in common with the word meal but the letter "a." Unlikely, in Arabic, all word classes are relatively similar. Consequently, those who learn the least number of Arabic words turn out to find themselves have, in fact, gained a lot of helpful words in no time.

The Arabic language belongs to the Bantu Family (African) languages spoken mostly in eastern, central, and southern Africa. Due to historical and political reasons, the language has borrowed heavily from Persian, Indian, and English. Slight borrowings from other languages might as well be found in Arabic, such as German and Portuguese. While the vocabulary is of mixed origins, the language syntax and grammar are purely Bantu and African. For centuries, Arabic remained the language of the people of the East African coast. However, that is only to say about Standard Arabic.

Standard Arabic is the official language used in any formal written document. It is used for all governmental purposes across the Arabian world. It is also the language spoken and written in all national and international newspapers and TV channels. On the contract, there are local dialects of Arabic that differ highly or slightly in the way they are pronounced. Furthermore, each country might have a wide set of sub-dialects. In brief, Standard Arabic is for all; a local dialect if for one.

Trade and migration from the Arabic coast during the nineteenth century helped to spread the language to different parts around the world. And since Arabians used to be innovative in so many fields such as medicine, math, astronomy, and philosophy; learning the Arabic language was – and still is – very tempting to other travelers to be able to get the most of its culture. In fact, it is called "The Arabian world" because the language has been widely used in African and the Asian continent.

During colonial times, as in all war times, missions tended to learn their enemies' language. The Arabian world was highly targeted because of its riches. Therefore, on average, the majority would learn Arabic instead of forcing the Arabs to learn their language for communication purposes with the local inhabitants.

Out of the languages spoken in eastern Africa, Arabic is the most used language. It is one of the languages that feature in some world radio stations such as the BBC, Radio Cairo (Egypt), the Voice of America (U.S.A.), Radio Deutsche Welle (Germany), Radio Moscow International (Russia), Radio Japan International, Radio China International, Radio Sudan, and Radio South Africa.

The Arabic language also makes its presence in the art world – in songs, theaters, movies, and television programs. For example, the popular Disney movie, "The Lion King" featured several Arabic words, such as "Rafiki" (friend), as the name of one character. Although many debate that Arabic is one of the most difficult languages to learn – to which experts absolutely disagree – it is promoted to be taught in many parts of the world. Subsequently, the number of Arabic learners has been increasing so far.

Due to the high demand for learning Arabic, learning resources vary. In a sense, it is all up to the learner to decide why and how they prefer to learn Arabic. As it has been, this guide is perfectly suitable for learning basic Arabic vocabulary and phrases to help the learner begin and manage a proper conversation with any native Arabian citizen. This guide serves ideally as a quick guideline to understanding "Why Arabic?", how to get started, and how to level up your Arabic language in the least possible time.

CHAPTER ONE:
LETTERS AND SOUNDS

Alphabets

Arabic uses its own alphabet. It could be fairly said that this is the reason why it had multiple loanwords, or borrowings, from other languages – because other languages gave simpler alternatives to some Arabic words. At length, other languages imported Arabic loanwords using English or Latin alphabet to write them down. Thus, the borrowing process has been reciprocal, which makes Arabic pronunciation reasonably easy. Nowadays, we call similar a process transliteration.

The pronunciation of a word can in most cases easily be seen from the way it is written.

On average, most words are pronounced the way they are written. In that, Arabic has no exceptions. For further explanation, in English, a word like "reign" has a silent (g) and it is pronounced as /rein/. Nonetheless, that does not happen in Arabic; all letters shall be turned into sounds. In addition, each letter represents a specific sound. The pronunciation of a sound does not change according to the context; it remains the same. That is why experts agree that Arabic reading and speaking is practically unmistakable and easy to learn once one learns the alphabet.

The Arabic alphabet consists of 27 letters, and they are as follows:

أ	ب	ت	ث	ج	ح	خ	د	ذ	ر	ز	س
A	B	t	Th (Think)	G (girl)	ha	kh	D	Th (Though)	R	z	S
ش	ص	ض	ط	ظ	ع	غ	ف	ق	ك	ل	م
Sh	S	D	T	Z	E	Gh	F	Q	K	L	M
ن	ه	و	ي								
N	H	W	Y								

Just like it is with most languages learning, the best way to practice pronunciation is to listen to Arabic audio materials or blend in with native Arabic speakers.

Vowels and syllable structure

Vowels are called **"El-la"** letters in Arabic. There are only three letters: a $(ا)$, w $(و)$, y $(ي)$. Unlike English, they are not complicated at all, neither in writing nor in pronunciation. Their pronunciation is fixed, and the same can be said about their function.

Surprisingly as it may seem, the Arabic language gives vowels slight to no importance. Arabic words may contain no vowels at all. Consequently, although many try to force syllable structure into the process of learning Arabic, Arabic linguists find it ultimately unnecessary.

On the other side, there is Harakat, which is the Arabic word for "moves." In English, it takes a vowel to change the way we pronounce a word, whereas in Arabic, it takes Harakat. These Harakat are Fatha, Kasra, and Damma. These Harakat function as little vowels. In addition, they are written in small figures, or they may not be written at all – once a learner feels he/she no longer needs them to read properly.

For example,

In English, the way we pronounce the /s/ differs according to the following vowel as follows:

S/a/nd
S/o/ld
S/e/ll

In Arabic, vowels are real letters. If they exist in the written form of the word, they are to be pronounced. If they do not exist, they are not to be pronounced. And from this point, we may use Harakat to produce connected speech as follows:

سَأل fatha ($\overset{-}{\circ}$) as seen above the $(ــس)$. Fatha functions as the vowel /a/.

سِليم Kasra ($\underset{\circ}{}$) as seen under the $(ــس)$. Kasra functions as the vowel /e/.

سُعاد Damma ($\overset{\circ}{}$) as seen above the $(ــس)$. Damma functions as the vowel /u/.

Beginners might use Harakat to learn how to read properly. Yet, if the learners begin with learning speaking and listening skills first, they will – most likely – not need to use Harakat to read properly because they will be able to tell – by common sense – which Harakat are to be used and where.

Here's a list of how to pronounce different letters using the three little Harakat or the three big vowels:

Sounds Represented by Letters	Letters with the three little Harakat (Or the three big vowels – if any)		
A	AA	EE	OO
B	BA	BE	BU
C	CA	CE	CU
F	FA	FE	FU
G	GA	GE	GU
GH	GHA	GHE	GHU
H	HA	HE	HU
J	JA	JE	JU
K	KA	KE	KU
KH	KHA	KHE	KHU
L	LA	LE	LU
M	MA	ME	MU
N	NA	NE	NU
P	PA	PE	PU
R	RA	RE	RU
S	SA	SE	SU
SH	SHA	SHE	SHU
T	TA	TE	TU
TH	THA	THE	THU
V	VA	VE	VU
W	WA	WE	WU
Y	YA	YE	YU
Z	ZA	ZE	ZU

Note that the letter "A" is the one that changes completely if added to Harkat since it is already a vowel.

CHAPTER TWO:
GREETINGS

Regardless of whether we are interacting with people we know or people we meet for the first time, the first thing we always do is greet them. That is why learning how to greet people in the target language is highly critical.

A language is a tool of communication. Subsequently, to communicate with people properly, we must learn the basics of how to conduct a decent conversation from greeting and till goodbye.

In the previous chapter, you learned about Arabic letters and sounds. The sounds will help you in good pronunciation of Arabic words. In this chapter, you will learn some of the common Arabic greetings, their translation, and transliteration in English.

General greetings that works very well for all possible occasions are:

	English	Arabic	Transliteration
Greeting	Hello	مرحباً	mar'ha'ban
Response	Hey	أهلاً	ahlan

Other phrases that you can use as greetings may include:

	English	Arabic	Transliteration
Greeting	Welcome to our home/country!	مرحباً بك في بلدنا	mar'ha'ban beka fe bala'de'na
Response	Thank you!	شكراً لك	shokran lak
	Welcome home! (At person's house)	مرحباً بك في منزلنا	mar'ha'ban beka fe man'zele'na

	Welcome, have a seat!	أهلاً، تفضل بالجلوس	ahlan, ta'fa'dal bel'joloso
	Thank you! /Thank you very much!	شكراً	shokran
	Goodbye!	مع السلامة	ma'a al'salama
Response	Goodbye! See you later!	مع السلامة، نراك لاحقاً	ma'a al'salama naraka lahe'qan
	Good morning!	صباح الخير	sabah al'khair
	Good evening	مساء الخير	masaa' al'khair
	Good day	نهارك سعيد	naharak Sa'eed
	How are you?	كيف حالك؟	kaif halok?
	I am good	أنا بخير	ana bikhayr
	How is everything?	كيف الأحوال؟	kaif Al'ahwal?
	What's up?	ماذا الجديد؟	mal jadeed
	Long time, no see	مر وقت طويل	mar'ra waqt taweel
	Excuse me	عذراً	Ozran
	Hello, my name is…	مرحباً، اسمي…	marhaban, ismi…
	See you later	أراك لاحقاً	araka laheqan
	See you tomorrow	أراك غداً	araka ghadan
	Let us meet again	لنلتقِ مجدداً	le'naltaqi mogadadan
	Have a good day	يوما سعيدًا	yawman sa'eedan
	Have a good night	ليلةً سعيدة	laylatan sa'eedatan
	Sleep well	نوماً هنيئاً	nawman ha'ne'an
	How is your day?	كيف يسير يومك؟	kaif yaseer yawmok?
	What's new?	ما الجديد؟	ma al'gadeed?
	How is life?	كيف تسير الحياة معك؟	kaif taseer al'haya ma'ak?
	Nice to see you	سررتُ برؤيتك	So'rer'to be'ro'yatek
	Nice to meet you	سررتُ بلقائك	So'rer'to be'leqa'ek
	How have you been?	كيف كان حالك؟	kaif kan halok?

	Hello everyone!	مرحباً بالجميع!	marhaban Jamee'an
	How are you feeling?	كيف تشعر؟	kaif tash'or?

Introducing yourself

Introducing yourself is very important. However, it may be used interchangeably with greeting. The difference would lie on whether you would like to let the one you are talking to more information about yourself or not.

It is – certainly – important that you keep sensitive information for yourself. Yet, it is highly recommended that you learn how to tell others to understand your situation in general.

By nature, there are two ways of introducing yourself: a formal and informal way – depending on the situation. Introductions are sometimes – if not all the time – accompanied with greetings in terms of showing a friendly attitude or as a matter of breaking the ice and expecting an interaction with your speech.

Nevertheless, the simpler, the better. In a sense, the main greeting to be used with self-introductions would be *"marhaban"* meaning "hello."

English	Arabic	Transliteration
My name is…	أنا اسمي...	ana ismi
What is your name?	ما اسمك؟	ma is'mok?
I am from America	أنا من أمريكا	ana men amreica
I am a student	أنا طالب	ana taleb
Where are you from?	من أيّ بلد أنت؟	men ayee baladen ant?
Pleased to meet you	سررتُ بلقائك	so'rer'to be'leka'ek
I work for…	أنا أعمل لصالح...	ana a'mal le'saleh…

Sometimes following our self-introduction, we might be asked a few important questions concerning our ability to communicate with others. Here is a list of commonly used sentences for such situations:

English	Arabic	Transliteration
Do you speak Arabic?	هل تتحدث اللغة العربية؟	hal ta'ta'hadath al'arabiya?
Just a little bit!	أتحدثها قليلاً	ata'hada'tho'ha qa'lilan
No! I don't speak Arabic. I speak English.	لا، لا أتحدث العربية. أنا أتحدث الإنجليزية	aa, la ata'hadath al'arabiya. Ana ata'hadath al engli'zi'ya
What is your name?	ما اسمك؟	ma is'mok?
My name is Adam.	اسمي آدم	ismi adam
Where are you from?	من أين أنت؟	men ayn ant?
I am from the United States of America.	أنا من أمريكا	ana men amrica
When did you arrive here?	متى وصلت إلى هنا؟	mata wasalta ela hona?
I arrived here about two weeks ago.	وصلتُ منذ حوالي أسبوعين	Wasalatu mondhu hawalay osobu'ayn
What do you do for a living?	ماذا تعمل؟	maza ta'mal?
Are you here on business or on a visit?	هل أنت هنا من أجل العمل أم للسياحة؟	hal anta hone men agl al'amal am ll'seyaha?
I am just visiting.	أنا هنا في زيارة وحسب	ana hona fe zi'yara wa'hasb

I live here.	أنا أعيش هنا	ana a'esh hone
How many years have you lived here?	منذ متى تعيش هنا؟	monz mata ta'esh hona?
I have lived here for six years.	أعيش هنا منذ ستة أعوام	a'eesh hona mondhu sittaty aa'wam
I'm pleased to know you.	أنا مسرور بمعرفتك	ana masrooron be'ma'refa'tek
I'm pleased to meet you.	أنا مسرور بلقائك	ana masrooron be'leqa'ek
We will meet later.	سنلتقي لاحقًا	sanaltaki laheqan

VOCABULARY FOR DIRECTIONS

Vocabulary for directions are the most important ones to learn. Simply because it is most likely that you desire to go to a place or ask for a certain location. In addition, they are very easy to learn, and they are also straightforward.

English	Arabic	Transliteration
Right	يمين	ya'meen
Left	يسار	ya'sar
Turn	انعطف	in'aa'tef
Cross the street	اعبر الطريق	o'bor al'tareq
Continue down	استمر في السير	ista'mer fel'sair
Go straight ahead	اذهب مباشرة	izhab mo'ba'shara'tan
Follow this road	اتبع هذا الطريق	it'ba haza al'tareq
Crossroad/Junction	تقاطع طُرق	taqat'oo toroq

Chapter Three: Numbers

In Arabic, it is very easy to count from 0 to 10. Like most languages, numbers from 0 to 10 are presented by a single word each.

English	Arabic	Transliteration
0	صِفر	sefr
1	واحد	wahed
2	اثنان	ith'nan
3	ثلاثة	tha'la'tha
4	أربعة	ar'ba'aa
5	خمسة	khamsa
6	ستة	set'ta
7	سبعة	sa'baa
8	ثمانية	tha'ma'neya
9	تسعة	tes'aa
10	عشرة	ash'ra

Note that all /th/ sounds in the numbers' transliterations are pronounced as those in the word "thank" not like those in the word "this."

English	Arabic	Transliteration
20	عشرون	ish'ron
30	ثلاثون	tha'la'thon
40	أربعون	ar'ba'oon
50	خمسون	khamson
60	ستون	set'ton
70	سبعون	sa'bon

80	ثمانون	tha'ma'non
90	تسعون	tes'on
100	مائة	ma'aa
1000	ألف	a'lf
10000	عشرة آلاف	ashart alaf
100,000 (One hundred thousand)	مائة ألف	meet alf
1,000,000 (One million)	مليون	million
10,000,000 (Ten million)	عشرة ملايين	ashrat malayeen
100,000,000 (One hundred million)	مائة مليون	meet malyoon
1,000,000,000 (One billion)	مليار	mil'yar

To get combined numbers, there are fixed rules to follow:

1. **Numbers from 11 to 19**

We simply place the number we want +10 (Ashar) as follows:

English	Arabic	Transliteration
11	أحد عشر/إحدى عشر	ahada ashar
12	اثنا عشر	ithna ashar
13	ثلاثة عشر	thalathata ashar
14	أربعة عشر	arb'aata ashar
15	خمسة عشر	kham'sata ashar
16	ستة عشر	set'tata ashar
17	سبعة عشر	sab'aata ashar
18	ثمانية عشر	thamanyata ashar
19	تسعة عشر	tes'aata ashar

2. Numbers up to 99

To get combined numbers up to 99, all you need is to add numbers from the first table to numbers from the second table using the letters and sound **"wa"** which means "and. " For example, to say "ninety-nine" in Arabic, you say nine and ninety or *"tes'as wa tes'on."*

Here's a list with more examples:

English	Arabic	Transliteration
21	واحد وعشرون	wahed **wa** Ish'ron
32	اثنان وثلاثون	ithnan **wa** Tha'la'thon
44	أربعة وأربعون	arba'a **wa** Ar'ba'oon
56	ستة وخمسون	set'ta **wa** Khamson
66	ستة وستون	set'ta **wa** Set'ton
76	ستة وسبعون	set'ta **wa** Sa'bon
83	ثلاثة وثمانون	thalatha **wa** Tha'ma'non
95	خمسة وتسعون	khamsa **wa** Tes'on
78	ثمانية وسبعون	thama'nya **wa** sa'bon

3. The number one hundred and its multiples

The numbers 100 and 200 are the only exception to this rule as they have fixed names regardless of the rule. 100 is known as *"ma'ah,"* and 200 is *"ma'a'tain."* Other multiples are formed by adding the first number from the first table, and then the word *"ma'ah"* as follows:

English	Arabic	Transliteration
300	ثلاثمائة	thalath **ma'ah**
400	أربعمائة	arb'aa **ma'ah**
500	خمسمائة	kham'sa **ma'ah**
600	ستمائة	set'ta **ma'ah**
700	سبعمائة	sab'aa **ma'ah**

| 800 | ثمانمائة | thamani **ma'ah** |
| 900 | تسعمائة | tes'o **ma'ah** |

The same can be said about the number 1000 and its multiples. The numbers 1000 and 2000 are the only exception to this rule as they have fixed names regardless of the rule.

1000 is known as **"alf,"** and 200 is **"alfain."** Other multiples are formed by adding the first number from the first table and then the word **"alaf"** as follows:

English	Arabic	Transliteration
3000	ثلاثة آلاف	thalathat *alaf*
4000	أربعة آلاف	arb'aat *alaf*
5000	خمسة آلاف	kham'sat *alaf*
6000	ستة آلاف	set'tat *alaf*
7000	سبعة آلاف	sab'aat *alaf*
8000	ثمانية آلاف	thamaniat *alaf*
9000	تسعة آلاف	tes'at *alaf*

Numbers combinations that consist of 100 and its multiples are formed by following the exact opposite of the previous case. In this case, we will place the number one hundred or its multiples first. Then, we will place other numbers. For example, to say 113, we combine one hundred and then 13 using the letters and sound **"wa"** which means "and." Therefore, 113 in Arabic would be "100+13" or **"ma'ah wa thalathat ashar."**

And to say 1011 would be 1000+11 or **"alf wa ahad ashar."**

Percentages

Percentages in Arabic do not drift away from the basic numbering. The only thing that changes when referring to percentages is the word percent. Percent is translated as **"be'ma'ah."** Therefore, it will be more of a direct translation from Arabic to English.

For example:

English	Arabic	Transliteration
1% – One percent	واحد بالمائة	wahed *bel'ma'ah*
2% – Two percent	اثنان بالمائة	ithnan *bel'ma'ah*
50% – Fifty percent	خمسون بالمائة	khamsoon *bel'ma'ah*
100% – One hundred percent	مائة بالمائة	ma'ah *bel'ma'ah*

The rest of the numbers follow the same pattern.

Fractions

Whether you are in the stock market or in the supermarket, you might need to use fractions. Fractions are different from the basic numbering. Like English, Arabic has unique terms that refer to different fractions. In English ¼ is a quarter, ½ a half and ¾ three-quarters.

English	Arabic	Transliteration
¼ quarter	ربع	Rob'ee
½ half	نصف	nos
¾ three-quarters.	ثلاثة أرباع	thalathat arba'a

How much, how often?

To talk about the number of times we carry out something, we use the word "mar'rah" after the number. Just like most of the rules, numbers 1 and 2 are always unique. To say "once," we say "mar'rah." To say "twice," we use *"mar'ra'tain."*

Other than that, we use the plural form of the word *"mar'rah"* which is *"mar'rat"* to express the rate of occurrence in accordance with other numbers. For example,

Three times is *"thalathat mar'rat."*

Four times is *"arba'at mar'rat,"* and the rest of the numbers follow the same pattern.

CHAPTER FOUR:
CALENDAR

In a nutshell, this chapter will help you learn about months of the year (*shohoor al'sana*), days of the week (*Ayam al'osboo*), and time (*wa'qt*).

Months of the year

The months are referred to using words that seem borrowed as follows:

English	Arabic	Transliteration
January	يناير	yana'yer
February	فبراير	feb'rayer
March	مارس	mares
April	أبريل	ebril
May	مايو	mayo
June	يونيو	yon'yo
July	يوليو	yol'yu
August	أغسطس	oghos'tos
September	سبتمبر	seb'tam'ber
October	أكتوبر	octobar
November	نوفمبر	novimber
December	ديسمبر	december

Days of the week

The week (*osbo*) in the Arabic world, just like in the West, has seven days (*ayam*). However, the work week in Arabic is from Sunday to Thursday; and weekends are Friday and Saturday. The names for Thursday (*Al'khamis*) and Friday (*Al'jum'aa*) are of Arabic origin. For instance, *Alkhamis* comes from the Arabic word "*khamsa,*" which means five. Friday (*Al'jum'aa*) has sacred importance in the Islamic religion. Here are the days of the week:

English	Arabic	Transliterations
Sunday	الأحد	al'ahad
Monday	الاثنين	al'ethnain
Tuesday	الثلاثاء	al'tho'la'thaa
Wednesday	الأربعاء	al'arba'aa
Thursday	الخميس	al'khamis
Friday	الجمعة	al'jum'aa
Saturday	السبت	al'sabt

Chapter Five: Colors

If you have reached this section, then congratulations! You are doing very well! You are now able to name months of the year, days of the week and numbers in Arabic.

This chapter will help you learn about colors. The table below shows the translation of basic colors to help you in your descriptions within a conversation in Arabic. In fact, it is sometimes very efficient to refer to an object using its color. For example, in Egypt, it is very common to use red to refer to tomatoes.

English	Arabic	Transliterations
White	أبيض	abyad
Gray	رمادي	ramady
Black	أسود	aswad
Brown	بُني	bon'ni
Red	أحمر	ah'mar
Orange	برتقالي	bor'to'kali
Yellow	أصفر	asfar
Blue	أزرق	az'rak
Purple	بنفسجي	banfsaji
Pink	وردي	wardi

Gold	ذهبي	za'ha'bi

Chapter Six: Animals and Insects

This chapter might be a practical or a humorous one based on why you would be interested in it.

As obvious as it is, many people are highly interested in visiting Africa for Safari reasons. Therefore, they like to learn some animals' names in Arabic. However, others learn the names of the animals to be able to escape from them or at the safest estimate, avoid them. Most of the animals' names are very similar to their English meaning. Subsequently, this chapter is expected to be easy and fun to learn.

Here you will learn about the most common animals in Arabic as follows:

English (Singular)	Arabic	Transliteration
Animal	حيوان	haya'wan
Ant	نملة	namla
Baboon	قردوح	kardoh
Bear	دب	dob
Bird	طائر	ta'er
Buffalo	جاموس	gamos
Butterfly	فراشة	fa'ra'sha
Cat	قِط	ket
Cheetah	فهد	fahd

Chicken	دجاجة	dajaja
Chimpanzee	شمبانزي	champanzy
Cockroach	صرصور	sarsor
Cow	بقرة	baqara
Crocodile	تمساح	tem'sah
Deer	غزال	ghazal
Dog	كلب	kalb
Donkey	حمار	hemar
Duck	بطة	bat'ta
Elephant	فيل	feel
Fish	سمكة	sama'ka
Fly	ذبابة	thoba'ba (th sound, as in "this")
Giraffe	زرافة	za'ra'fa
Goat	ماعز	ma'ez
Grasshopper	جراد	ja'rad
Hippopotamus	فرس النهر	faras Al nahr
Horse	حصان	hesan
Hyena	ضبع	dab'
Impala	ظبي	zabi

Insect	حشرة	ha'sha'ra
Leopard	نمر	nemr
Lion	أسد	asad
Monkey	قرد	kerd
Mouse	فأر	fa'r
Ostrich	نعامة	na'ama
Parrot	ببغاء	bba'ghaa
Peacock	طاووس	tawoos
Pig	خنزير	khan'zeer
Python	أصَلة	asala
Rabbit	أرنب	arnab
Rhinoceros	وحيد القرن	waheed al'qarn
Shark	قرش	kersh
Sheep	خروف	kharoof
Snake	ثعبان	tho'ban (th sound, as in "thank")
Turkey	ديك رومي	deek romy
Turtle	سلحفاة	sol'ho'fat
Warthog	خنزير بري	khanzeer bar'ry
Whale	حوت	hoot

Zebra	حمار وحشي	hemar wah'shi

CHAPTER SEVEN: FAMILY AND RELATIONS

Sometimes, it is very important to either know or let others know the relationship between any two to eliminate any false suspicions (or confirm them). Arabians have some restrictions when it comes to relationships. Therefore, they value them. In this chapter, you will learn all possible relations in Arabic and according to the Arabic culture.

English	Arabic	Transliteration
Brother	أخ	akh
Stepbrother	أخ غير شقيق	akh ghair shaqiq
Sister	أخت	okht
Stepsister	أخت غير شقيقة	okht ghair shaqiqa
Sibling	شقيق	shaqiq
Daughter	ابنة	ibna
Son	ابن	ibn
Twins	توأم	taw'am
Father	أب	aab
Stepfather	زوج أم	zawj om
Mother	أم	om
Stepmother	زوجة أب	zawjat aab
Uncle (Maternal)	خال	khal

Uncle (Paternal)	عم	a'm
Aunt (Maternal)	خالة	kha'la
Aunt (Paternal)	عمة	am'ma
Child	طفل	tefl
Grandchild	حفيد	hafeed
Cousin (daughter/maternal)	ابنة خال	ibnat khal
Cousin (son/maternal)	ابن خال	ibn khal
Cousin (daughter/paternal)	ابنة عم	ibnat a'm
Cousin (son/paternal)	ابن عم	ibn a'm
Mother-in-law	حماة	ha'maa
Father-in-law	حما	ham'ma
Fiancée (lady)	خطيبة	khatiba
Fiancé (gentleman)	خطيب	khatib
Grandfather	جد	ja'd
Grandmother	جدة	jad'da
Nephew	ابن الأخ	ibn al'akh
Niece	ابنة الأخت	ibnat al'okht
Husband	زوج	zawj
Wife	زوجة	zawja

Sister-In-Law (Husband's sister / Wife's sister)	أخت الزوج/ أخت الزوجة	okht ezzooj/okht ezzooja
brother-In-Law (Husband's brother / Wife's brother)	أخ الزوج/ أخ الزوجة	akh ezzouj / akh ezzouja
Friend	صديق	sa'deek

As you might have noticed, normally all female titles end in a taa' (ة), which is expressed with /a/ at the end of the word in the transliteration column. And this letter is what marks feminine words in Arabic.

CHAPTER EIGHT:
SHOPPING, MONEY, AND IMPORTANT PLACES

Business forms a necessary part of any society. It is technically impossible to travel to a country without having to discuss money. Therefore, this chapter is dedicated to exposing you to some basic terms and phrases which will be helpful in different business situations in general.

Arabic	English	Transliteration
Money	نقود	nokood
Pound	جنيه	jeneh
Dollar	دولار	do'lar
Cent	قرش	kersh
Butchery	الجزارة	jez'ara
Price	سعر	se'r
Cheap	رخيص	rakhis
Expensive	غالي	ghali
Buy	شراء	she'ra
Sell	بيع	bai'
Okay	حسناً	ha'sa'nan
No	لا	la
Market	سوق	souq

Store	متجر	mat'gar
Grocery shop	محل البقالة	mahal el'be'qala
Bookstore	متجر الكتب	mat'gar al'kotob
Shopkeeper	صاحب المتجر	saheb al'mat'gar
Half	نصف	nesf
Size	مقاس	makas
Kilo	كيلو	kilo
How much? (price)	كم ثمن؟	kam thaman (th sound, as in "thank")
Price	ثمن	thaman
How many?	كم عدد؟	kam adad

Important Places

English	Arabic	Transliteration
Mosque	مسجد	masjed
Church	كنيسة	kanesa
Market	سوق	souq
Home	منزل	manzel
Bathroom (Toilet)	حمام	ham'mam
Kitchen	مطبخ	mat'bakh

Garden	حديقة	hadeqa
Hospital	مستشفى	mos'tash'fa
School	مدرسة	mad'rasa
Police station	قسم الشرطة	kesm eshorta

CHAPTER NINE: TECHNOLOGY

Since most of the Arabian world depends – to an extent – on imported technology, some technological terms have been borrowed from English, which make it easy to master technological terms in Arabic. Therefore, most technology-related terms are identical to those in English. For example, "fax" and "computer" are both pronounced exactly as fax and computer. However, other words may use the two variants of both English and Arabic. For example, the word "mobile" is either known as "mobile" or its Arabic meaning **"hatef."** In addition, the word "message" is either called "message" or **"resalla."**

Currently, there is no general rule for whether to use English or Arabic terms to describe words. It is all up to the speaker's preferences. However, according to statistics provided by users, there is a tendency to follow the majority's trend to determine only one term for each object in the future. Nevertheless, new linguistic developments in the language gradually come with new terminologies to make the language as independent as possible.

Here's a list of some common words used in this context:

English	Arabic	Transliteration
Speaker	مكبر الصوت	mukabber essot
Processor (in the computer)	معالج	mu'alej
Screen	شاشة	shasha
Monitor	شاشة حاسوب	shashat el hasoob
Keyboard	لوحة المفاتيح	lawhat el mafa'teeh
Mouse	فأرة	fa'rah
Microphone	ميكروفون	microphone
Laptop	حاسوب محمول	hasub mahmool

Printer	طابعة	tabi'aa
Mobile Phone	هاتف محمول	hatef mahmool
Internet	إنترنت	internet
Email	بريد إلكتروني	email

Office

Depending on the English borrowings for technology-related terminologies and since business is a global niche, it can be fairly said that the number of borrowings in the business area is significant. Subsequently, a foreigner who speaks English might find himself/herself able to establish communication with native Arabic speakers without having to talk much Arabic. Here's a list of the most common words to use in the office context:

As you will notice, most of them are English borrowings.

English	Arabic	Transliteration
Board (as in 'board of directors')	مجلس	majless
Meeting	إجتماع	ijtimaa
Conference	مؤتمر	mo'tamar
Cabinet	مكتب إدارة	maktab idary
Book	كتاب	ketab
Office	مكتب	office
Messenger	ماسنجر	messenger
Chair	كرسي	korsi
Officer	ضابط	dabet
Paper	ورق	wa'raq
Clerk	موظف	mo'wa'zaf
Pen	قلم	ka'lam
Computer	كمبيوتر/حاسوب	computer
Pencil	قلم رصاص	ka'lam rosas
Computer monitor	شاشة حاسوب	shashat el hasoob
Photocopy	نسخة	nos'kha

Conference room	غرفة المؤتمر	ghorfat al mo'tamar
Printer	طابعة	tabi'aa
Director	مدير	mo'deer
Record book	السِّجِل	segel
Report	تقارير	taqa'reer
Fax machine	فاكس	fax
Secretary	أمين عام	secretariaa
File	ملف	file
Shelf	رَف	raf
Folder	ملف	ma'laf
Supervisor	مُشرف	mosh'ref
Janitor	عامل نظافة	amel na'za'fa
Table	طاولة	ta'wela
Desk	طاولة	tawela
Letter	رسالة	resala
Manager	مدير	mo'deer
Work	عمل	a'mal
Worker	عامل	aa'mel
Job	وظيفة	wa'ze'fa

Using a telephone

English	Arabic	Transliteration
Telephone	هاتف	hatef
Is there a telephone here?	هل يوجد هاتف هنا؟	hal yojad hatef hona?
Where is the telephone?	أين الهاتف؟	ayn al' hatef?
I want to use a telephone	أريد استخدام الهاتف	oreed istekhdam al' hatef
Just for a minute	دقيقة فقط	daqeqa fa'qat
A short call	مكالمة قصيرة	moka'lama qasera
A long call	مكالمة طويلة	moka'lama tawela
I will pay for it	سأدفع ثمنها (/ثمنه)	sa'adfaa tha'man'aha (th sound, as in "thank")
Thank you	شكراً لك	shokran lak

CHAPTER TEN:
COURTESY AND EMERGENCY

Although it rarely happens, it is very important to have some basic knowledge about urgent and dangerous situations. In this chapter, you will be exposed to some keywords which refer to the seriousness of a certain situation, an accident, a fire, and how to respond to each.

English	Arabic	Transliteration
Ambulance	سيارة إسعاف	sayarat isaf
Bathroom/Restroom	حمام	ham'mam
Run away!	اهرب	oh'rob
Danger	خطر	khatar
Fire	حريق	hareeq
Get out	اخرج	okhroj
Go away	ابتعد	ibta'ed
Medicine	دواء	da'waa
Help	مساعدة	mosa'ada
Who?	مَن؟	ma'n?
What?	ماذا؟	maza?
When?	متى؟	mata?
Where?	أين؟	ayn?
No!	لا!	la!
Yes	نعم	na'am
Which?	أي؟ / أية؟	ai?
May I come in?	هل يمكنني الدخول؟	hal yom'keno'ni eddokhol?

Goodbye	إلى اللقاء	ela leqaa
Thank you	شكراً لك	shokran lak
I'm sick	أنا مريض	ana mareed
I'm hurt	أنا مصاب	ana mo'saab
Please	من فضلك	men fadlek
Sorry (to apologize)	آسف	asif
Sorry (to sympathize)	لا تحزن	la tahzan

CHAPTER ELEVEN: QUESTION WORDS

Question words are highly important and yet super easy to learn because they function perfectly as a standalone. It is very common to ask a question using a question word alone. For example, when discussing a football match, it is mostly enough to ask "when?" instead of asking "when will the match begin?"

In that Arabian people – by nature – are concise and hasty. They tend to take words from the tip of a tongue instead of listening to the speaker's full speech. This applies to all sorts of speech and, therefore, questions. Questions include things, time, people, or place. Here's a list of the most common question words:

English	Arabic	Transliteration
Who?	مَن؟	ma'n?
What?	ماذا؟	maza?
Why?	لماذا؟	le'maza?
When?	متى؟	mata?
Where?	أين؟	ayn?
Whose?	لِمن؟	le'ma'n?

However, in case you would like to produce full sentences, the general rule to ask about actions is to place the verb after the question word. For example, "Why are you crying?" is translated literally as "Why crying?", which is *"Lema'za tabki?"* / لماذا تبكي؟

For more examples, you may check the following list:

English	Arabic	Transliteration
Why are you laughing?	لماذا تضحك؟	le'maza tadhak?
Where are you going?	أين تذهب؟	ayn tazhab?
When will you leave?	متى ستغادر؟	mata sa'to'ghader?
What are you doing?	ماذا تفعل؟	maza taf'al?
Who plays?	من يلعب؟	ma'n yal'ab?

The same might be said on questions about nouns, including people, objects, or places. You will simply place the noun after the question word. For example, "who will join?" would be **"ma'am yan'dam?"**/ مَن ينضم؟ Or literally "who join?" in Arabic.

English	Arabic	Transliteration
What does he say?	ماذا يقول؟	maza yakool?
Where are you going?	أين تذهب؟	ayn tazhab?
Who is here?	من هنا؟	ma'n hona?
When did he come here?	متى جاء؟	mata jaa'?
Why are you laughing?	لماذا تضحك؟	le'maza tadhak?

However, there's only one exception to this rule and that is "whose," for which we place the noun before *it*. You may check the following list for a better understanding.

English	Arabic	Transliteration
Whose child?	طفل من؟	tefl ma'n?

Whose children?	أطفال من؟	atfal ma'n?
Whose book?	كتاب من؟	ketab ma'n?
Whose books?	كتب من؟	kotob ma'n?

As you have noticed, no changes occur to the question word nor the question form in either singular or plural forms.

Asking the whereabouts of a person or thing

English	Arabic	Transliteration
Where is the railway station?	أين محطة القطار؟	ayn ma'hatat al'qetar?
It is in front of…	إنها أمام...	ina'ha amam…
Where is the teacher?	أين المُعلم؟	ayn al'mo'al'em
He / she's at school.	إنه/ إنها في المدرسة.	in'aho/in'aha fel'madrasa
Where are the students?	أين الطلاب؟	ayn al'tollab?
They're at home.	إنهم في المنزل	in'nahom fel'manzel

Yes or no questions

To create a yes or no question in Arabic, you will simply use the word **"hal"** which is equivalent to the verb (to be/to do) in English. For example, a question like "did you have lunch?" can be translated into

"hal tanawalta al'ghadaa?" / هل تناولت الغداء؟

And the answer is either "yes" or "no" as follows.

English	Arabic	Transliteration
Did you study?	هل ذاكرت؟/هل درست؟	hal zakart?
Yes	نعم	na'am
No	لا	la

Expressing your point of view

Here are some useful phrases to express your point of view:

English	Arabic	Transliteration
Agree	أتفق	ata'feq
Disagree	لا أتفق	la ata'feq
I agree with…	أتفق مع...	ata'feq ma'a…
I agree with you	أتفق معك	ata'feq ma'ak
I agree with him / her.	أتفق معه/ معها	ata'feq ma'aho/ ma'aha
I don't agree.	لا أتفق	la Ata'feq
I don't agree with…	لا أتفق مع...	la ata'feq ma'a…
I don't agree with you	لا أتفق معك	la ata'feq ma'ak
I don't agree with him / her	لا أتفق معه/ معها	la Ata'feq ma'aho/ ma'aha
Argue	يجادل	yo'ja'del
Why are we arguing?	لماذا نتجادل؟	le'maza nata'gadal?
Let's stop here	لنتوقف هنا	le'nata'waqaf hona

At this point, you may be wondering about the difference between confirmation and negation in Arabic. In case you did not notice it, the previous examples showed that using the word "la" changes the sentence's meaning from confirmation to negation. In a sense, this two-letter word "la" means "no." The literal translation of one of the previously mentioned sentences is:

I no agree (I don't agree).

Therefore, as a beginner, you may simply put "la" in front of any statement you would like to negate, and you will have successfully negated its meaning. However, kindly note that negating a negative is a confirmation. For example, when saying, "I do not like no banana," you are simply saying, "I like banana." It might slide in English but in Arabic, you must stress whether you are negating a sentence or confirming it.

Useful phrases and structures

English	Arabic	Transliteration
First, firstly	أولاً	awwa'lan
Then / later on	ثم، بعد ذلك	thom'ma (th sound, as in "thank")/ ba'ad zalek
Again, still	أيضاً، مع ذلك	aydan, ma'a zalek
Besides also apart/aside from	إلى جانب	ila ganeb zalek
Finally, in the end	أخيراً، في النهاية	akheeran, fe'elnehaya
Let alone, despite	مع ذلك	ma'a zalek
Instead of	بدلاً من ذلك	bada'lan men zalek
I also disagree	أنا أيضاً لا أتفق	ana aydan la Ata'feq
Are you sure?	هل أنت متأكد؟	hal Anta mota'ak'ked
Certainly	بالطبع	bettabaa
Without doubt	بلا شك	be'la shak

Well-wishing

English	Arabic	Transliteration
Congratulations	مُبارك	mobarak
Good luck	حظاً سعيداً	hazan sa'edan
Cheer up	تفاءل	ta'fa'al
Happy birthday!	عيد ميلاد سعيد	eid melad sa'eed
Best wishes	أطيب الأمنيات	atyab el'omni'yat

CHAPTER TWELVE: ACTION VERBS

Prefixes: Basics

In this chapter, you will be introduced to the basic prefixes needed to construct short sentences properly yet easily. In Arabic, there are multiple sentence structures. A sentence may be formed with or without a verb. A sentence might be either nominal or verbal. It might start with a verb or a noun. As complicated as it might seem, it is –in fact –pleasant information. In brief, it means that nearly all sentences a beginner construct will be considered as well-established sentences.

There is no such thing as irregular verbs in Arabic. Subsequently, all verbs in all tenses are somehow similar. The base remains the same. Yet, prefixes and suffixes are what differ – sometimes slightly, other times significantly. Primarily they modify verbs to show the subject, the tense, the gender of the subject, and the object of a sentence. They also modify other parts of speech, such as adjectives and possessives, to align with the nouns and pronouns used in the sentence. All in all, by practice, you will find it very easy to generalize a rule for prefixes and suffixes.

In the following pages, you will be introduced to all what it takes – one step at a time – to be able to produce perfectly constructed sentences. Each rule is to be followed by enough examples to elaborate it as easy as possible and as concise as desired.

English	Arabic	Transliteration
To write	يكتب	yaktob
To read	يقرأ	yakra
To be able	يستطيع	yasta'te
To buy	يشتري	yash'tari
To remove	يزيل	yozeel
To come	يأتي	ya'ti

To say	يقول	yaqool
To cook	يطهو	yat'hoo
To see	يرى	ya'raa
To sell	يبيع	ya'bee
To drink	يشرب	yash'rab
To sit	يجلس	yaj'les
To eat	يأكل	ya'kol
To sleep	ينام	ya'nam
To feel	يشعر	yash'or
To speak	يتحدث	ya'ta'hadath (th sound, as in "thank")
To give	يعطي	yo'ti
To stand up	يقف	ya'qef
To give out	يمنح	yam'nah
To think	يفكّر	yofakker
To go	يذهب	yaz'hab
To travel	يسافر	yo'safer
To hear	يسمع	yas'ma
To wake up	يستيقظ	yas'tai'qez
To laugh	يضحك	yad'hak
To cry	يبكي	yabki
To walk	يسير	yaseer
To like/to love	يُعجَب / يحب	yo'jab/Yoheb
To want	يريد	yoreed
To listen	يستمع	yastam'ae
To wash	يغسل	yaghsel
To look at	ينظر إلى	tanzor ela
To look for	يبحث عن	yab'hath aan (th sound, as in "thank")

To work	يعمل	ya'mal
To pay	يدفع	yadf'aa
To watch	يشاهد	yo'shahed

As shown, all verbs in their base form begin with the letter ي / Y, which is equivalent to the English "to." In that, it is readily conjugated with the pronouns "he" to express the present tense. In other words, to say that the third singular pronoun, "he" is doing any action from the above list, you will not change the verb form at all. For example,

The verb "to watch" is *"yo'shahed"* / يشاهد and "he" is *"ho'wa"* / هو

Therefore, the sentence becomes as follows:

"He watches TV": *ho'wa yo'shahed al'television* / هو يشاهد التلفزيون

"He works": *ho'wa ya'mal* / هو يعمل

"He is looking for the mobile phone": *ho'wa yab'hath aan al phone* / هو يبحث عن الفون.

On the other side, to conjugate these verbs with the third singular pronoun she, we replace the "Y"/ ي letter at the beginning of the verbs (the base form) with "T"/ ت

For example, the verb "to watch" is "to'shahed" / تشاهد and "she" is he'ya / هي

Therefore, the previous examples become as follows:

"She watches TV": he'ya to'shahed al'television / هي تشاهد التلفزيون

"She works": he'ya ta'mal / هي تعمل

"She is looking for the mobile phone": he'ya tab'hath aan al phone / هي تبحث عن الفون

Lastly, and most importantly, if you would like to speak for yourself or use the pronoun I, you will replace the "Y"/ ي letter at the beginning of the verbs (the base form) with "A" / أ

For example, the verb "to watch" is "o'shahed" and "I" is "ana" / أشاهد

Therefore, the previous examples become as follows:

"I watch TV": ana o'shahed al'television / أنا أشاهد التلفزيون

"I work": ana a'mal / أنا أعمل

"I am looking for the mobile phone": ana ab'hath aan al phone / أنا أبحث عن الفون

CHAPTER THIRTEEN: OTHER USEFUL PHRASES

Food

English	Arabic	Transliteration
Food	طعام	ta'am
Bread	خبز	khobz
Rice	أرز	a'roz
Macaroni	معكرونة	ma'ka'rona
Meat	لحم	lahm
Fish	سمك	sa'mak
Chicken	دجاج	da'jaj
Vegetables	خضراوات	khod'rawat
Fruit	فاكهة	fa'keha
Corn	ذرة	zo'ra
Sweets	حلوى	halwa
Dessert	تحلية	tah'liya
Soup	حساء	hasaa
Salad	سلطة	salata

Other useful expression in this context include:

English	Arabic	Transliteration
I am hungry	أشعر بالجوع	ash'or bel'jo
What kind of food is there today?	ما نوع الطعام الموجود اليوم؟	ma no'o al'taam al'mawjood hona al'yawm?

Today, there are potatoes, meat, and fruit	اليوم، يوجد بطاطا، لحم، وفاكهة	al'yawm, yojad batata, lahm, wa fakeha.
Can I get some salads?	هل يمكنني الحصول على بعض السلطة؟	hal yom'kenoni al'hosol ala baad essalata?
Certainly sir, you will get it	بالطبع سيدي، ستحصل عليها	bettab'ae saiedi, sa'tahsol alaiha
Bring me some carrots, please.	أحضر لي بعض الجزر، من فضلك	ahder lee ba'da al'jazar men fadlek
Beef	لحم بقري	lahm baqari
Mutton	لحم ضأن	lahm da'an
Pork	لحم خنزير	lahm khenzir
Chicken	دجاج	dajaj
Do you have roast meat here?	هل يوجد لحم مشوي هنا؟	hal yo'jad lahm mashwi hona?
Yes, we have…	نعم، يوجد	na'aam Yo'jad
How much do you want?	كم تريد؟	kam toreed?
Do they put in onions and pepper?	هل يضعون البصل والفلفل؟	hal yada'oon al'basal wa al'folfol?

Nevertheless, it is worth noting that most Arab countries do not serve pork nor tolerate having it – for religious reasons. Exceptions may be found in UAE and Lebanon since most of their population are either foreigner or non-Muslims.

Drinks/beverages

Learning how to order a drink is undoubtedly significant since some of them are to be drunk at a specific temperature. As a result, most people tend to buy them fresh. Arabian countries are mostly popular for their coffee and natural juices, and so here are some of words and expressions you may need:

English	Arabic	Transliteration
Water	ماء	ma'a
Tea	شاي	shai
Coffee	قهوة	qahwa
Milk	حليب	haleeb
Juice	عصير	aseer
Soda with ice	صودا بالثلج	soda bel'thalg (th sound, as in "thank")
Tea without milk	شاي بدون حليب	shai bedon haleeb
Ice Americano	أمريكانو مُثلج	americano mo'thal'lag (th sound, as in "thank")
Beer	بيرة	Beera
Whisky	ويسكي	Wiski

It is also worth noting that most Arab countries do not serve beer, whiskey, or any spiritual drinks; nor tolerate having them – for religious reasons. Exceptions may be found in UAE and Lebanon since most of their population are either foreigner, non-Muslims, or both.

Asking about the time

English	Arabic	Transliteration
What's the time?	كم الساعة؟	kam essa'aa?
What time is it now?	كم الساعة الآن؟	kam essa'aa al'aan?
The time is . . .	الساعة....	assa'aa...
The time now is . . .	الساعة الآن....	assa'aa al'aan...

The time now is seven o'clock in the evening	الساعة الآن السابعة مساءًا	assa'aa al'aan assabe'aa masa'aan
The time now is twelve o'clock in the daytime (noon)	الساعة الآن الثانية عشرة ظهراً	assa'aa al'aan athaneyata ashrata thohran (th sound, as in "the")

Asking what somebody is doing

English	Arabic	Transliteration
What are you doing? (Addressing a singular subject)	ماذا تفعل؟	maza taf'al?
I am working.	أنا أعمل	a'na a'mal
What are you doing? (Addressing a plural subject)	ماذا تفعلون؟	maza taf'alon?
We are studying.	نحن ندرس	nahno nadros

Pronouns

The first thing to learn when constructing a sentence is pronouns. As you will see, they are slightly different from those in English. However, the difference lies only in terms of usage such as singular or plural and masculine or feminine. In Arabic, there are two kinds of sentences: verbal phrases and nominal phrases. For nominal phrases, it is very common to start with a pronoun (any of them).

English	Arabic	Transliteration
I	أنا	ana
We	نحن	nahno
You (Singular)	أنت	anta
You (Plural)	أنتم	antom
They	هم	hom
He	هو	ho'wa

She	هي	he'ya
It	هو / هي	ho'wa/he'ya

Notes to consider:

1. In Arabic, the pronoun "you" has two variants: singular and plural.
2. In Arabic, the pronoun "it" comes in two forms: a feminine and a masculine one depending on the genre it describes. The masculine form of "it" is identical to "he" whereas the feminine form of "it" is identical to "she."

Talking about nationality

English	Arabic	Transliteration
I am a Tanzanian.	أنا تنزاني	ana tenzani
I am a European.	أنا أوروبي	ana orobi
I am an American.	أنا أمريكي	ana ame'riki
I am a Kenyan.	أنا كيني	ana keni
I'm a Frenchman	أنا فرنسي	ana frensi
I'm an Egyptian	أنا مصري	ana mesri
I am Swedesh	أنا سويدي	ana swedi
I am Japanese	أنا ياباني	ana yabani
I am Chinese	أنا صيني	ana seeni
I am German	أنا ألماني	ana almani
I am Somali	أنا صومالي	ana somali
I am an Indian	أنا هندي	ana hendi

As shown, to talk about nationality in Arabic, the general rule says to place the possessive Y / ي at the end of the country's name. In a sense, it is more like "this country is mine" than it is "I come from this country."

Countries

English	Arabic	Transliteration
America	أمريكا	amrica
Holland	هولندا	hollanda
Germany	ألمانيا	almania
Belgium	بلجيكا	beljika
Mozambique	موزمبيق	mozambiq
Canada	كندا	canada
Egypt	مصر	misr
England	إنجلترا	engiltra

Asking where someone comes from

English	Arabic	Transliteration
Where do you come from? (singular)	من أين أنت؟	men ayn ant?
Where do you come from? (plural)	من أين أنتم؟	men ayn antom?
Where do they come from?	من أين هم؟	men ayn hom?

Saying where you stay/where you reside

English	Arabic	Transliteration
I live in Mombasa	أنا أعيش في مومباسا	ana a'eesh fe mombasa
I live in Tanzania	أنا أعيش في تنزانيا	ana a'eesh fe tenzania
I live in America	أنا أعيش في أمريكا	ana a'eesh fe Amrica
I live in a hotel	أنا أعيش في فندق	ana a'eesh fe fondoq
I live in a big building	أنا أعيش في مبنى كبير	ana a'eesh fe mabna kabeer
I live in a fine house	أنا أعيش في منزل جيد	ana a'eesh fe manzel jai'yed

I live in a hostel	أنا أعيش في نُزُل صغير	ana a'eesh fe nozol sagheer
I live in my own house	أنا أعيش في منزلي الخاص	ana a'eesh fe manzeli al'khas
I am living in a village	أنا أعيش في قرية	ana a'eesh fe kar'ya
I am staying in a small house	أنا أعيش في منزل صغير	ana a'eesh fe manzel sagheer

Describing your means of transportation

English	Arabic	Transliteration
I come on foot	أنا آتي سيراً على الأقدام	ana aati sairan alal aqdam
I come by minibus	أنا آتي بالميكروباص	ana aati bel'microbas
I travel on foot	أنا أتنقل سيراً على الأقدام	ana atanaqal sairan alal aqdam
I travel by minibus	أنا أتنقل بالميكروباص	ana atanaqal bel'microbas
I travel by bus	أنا أتنقل بالحافلة	ana atanaqal bel'hafela
I travel by car	أنا أتنقل بالسيارة	ana atanaqal bel'sai'yara
I travel by train	أنا أتنقل بالقطار	ana atanaqal bel'qetar
I travel by bike	أنا أتنقل بالدراجة	ana atanaqal bel'dar'raja

Feeling hungry, thirsty, or full

English	Arabic	Transliteration
I feel hungry	أنا أشعر بالجوع	ana ash'or bel'jo
I am hungry	أنا جائع	ana Ja'ae
I feel thirsty	أنا أشعر بالعطش	ana ash'or bel'atash
I am thirsty	أنا عطشان	ana at'shan
I'm satisfied, I've had enough	أنا بخير، لقد شبعتُ	ana be'khair, lakad sha'bet
I am full	لقد شبعتُ	lakad sha'bet

Describing an illness

English	Arabic	Transliteration
I am sick	أنا مريض	ana mareed
I have a fever	لدي حمى	ladaya homma
I have a cold	لدي برد	ladaya bard
I am in pain	أنا أتألم	ana ata'alam
I have a stomachache	معدتي تؤلمني	ma'edati to'lemo'ni
I have a headache	لدي صداع	ladaya so'da
I am not feeling okay	لا أشعر أنني بخير	la ash'or anna'ni bekhair
I feel dizzy	أشعر بدوار	ash'or be'sodaa

Describing how you feel

To describe basic feelings, the following table will be useful. Yet, it is to be conjugated as previously explained according to the subject.

English	Arabic	Transliteration
Hear (verb)	يسمع	yas'ma
See (verb)	يرى	ya'ra
Feel (verb)	يشعر	yash'or
Cold (noun)	برد	bard
Hot	حر	har
Heat (noun)	حرارة	hara'ra
Understand (verb)	يفهم	yaf'ham

Examples in dialogue

English	Arabic	Transliteration
I feel cold	أنا أشعر بالبرد	ana ash'or bel'bard

I feel hot	أنا أشعر بالحر	ana ash'or bel'har

Body parts

English	Arabic	Transliteration
Shoulder	كتف	katef
Back	ظهر	zahr
Armpit	إبط	ibet
Stomach	معدة	ma'eda
Elbow	كوع	ko'o
Thumb	إبهام	ibham
Finger	إصبع	isba'a
Hand	يد	Yad
Fist	قبضة	Kabda
Buttocks	مؤخرة	mo'akhera
Arm	ذراع	Thera'a (th sound, as in "the")
Palm Of Hand	راحة اليد	rahat al'yad
Forearm	ساعِد	sa'ed
Waist	خصر	khasr
Wrist	مِعصم	me'sam
Leg	ساق	saq
Knee	ركبة	rokba
Hip	ورك	werk
Foot	قدم	kadam
Toe	إصبع قدم	isba' kadam
Heel	كعب	ka'b
Thigh	فخذ	fakhz
Ankle	كاحل	kahel

Conclusion

This beginners' guide is dedicated to help users in understanding and being understood in Arabian contexts. These areas include, but are not limited to, the Middle East, North Africa, East Africa, and Arabic speakers next door. It has been written concisely yet inclusively aiming to focus more on quality than quantity.

Mainly, this guide is expected, considered, and proved to be sufficient when it comes to everyday communication. This handbook gives tips on introducing yourself, getting simple directions, breaking the ice, purchasing items including meals and other products, communicating with the locals, and much more. This guide is dedicated to help users get the most out of every time they intend to communicate, while enjoying the process.

Review

This book has been made with passion — with the sole aim of bringing English speakers one step closer to Arabic culture through the means of a rich language that you can carry with you wherever you go and experience its magic unfold right in front of you.

If you found this book helpful in your travels, and if it helped you inch closer to grasping the vast sea of Arabic, head over to Amazon and leave a review about your experience. We would love to hear how your communication in Arabic unfolded with this book in your hands.

References

Alif (2022, May 16). How do you say simple sentences in Arabic in a common situation. Retrieved from

https://alifarabic.com/how-do-you-say-simple-sentences-in-arabic-in-a-common-situation/

A. P. (October 24, 2019). October 24, 2019. Hit the Ground Running with Arabic Numbers. Retrieved from

https://www.arabicpod101.com/blog/2019/10/24/arabic-numbers/

Azza H. (2022, September 18). Modern Standard Arabic Courses. Retrieved from
https://www.arabacademy.com/modern-standard-arabic-courses-we-offer/

Nadiia M. (2022, September 12). Challenge accepted: Getting to grips with basic Arabic grammar rules. Retrieved from

https://preply.com/en/blog/arabic-grammar-rules/

OptiLingo. (2022, April 5). All About Arabic Grammar. Retrieved from
https://www.optilingo.com/blog/arabic/all-about-arabic-grammar-and-verbs/

Made in United States
Troutdale, OR
12/08/2024

26104443R00038